Creative
Quilling

Creative Quilling

Traditional and modern designs

Trees Tra and Pieter van der Wolk

Kangaroo Press

Designer: Karel van Laar, de Bilt
Photography: Studio Koppelman, Maarssen
English translation: Tina Llowarch, Kenthurst

Opposite title page: Colour plate 1: Some examples of
modern paper quilling (page 47)

English translation © 1995 Kangaroo Press

Reprinted 1996
This edition first published in 1995
by Kangaroo Press Pty Ltd
3 Whitehall Road Kenthurst NSW 2156 Australia
PO Box 6125 Dural Delivery Centre NSW 2158
Printed in Hong Kong through Colorcraft Ltd

ISBN 0 86417 675 9

Contents

1 Quilled designs using paper strips of different widths

Introduction

This book, which follows on from *The Art of Quilling*, shows that the art of quilling need not be limited to the traditional—there are a number of applications using strips of paper which have not actually been thought of as quilling, which can extend the traditional.

We have included both traditional jewellery and modern designs in this book.

The diversity of colours available in quilling paper make possible designs suited to interior decoration, especially when the full length of the paper is used in larger, picture-sized works.

For the traditional designs we used for inspiration some old workbooks used by silversmiths on the art of silver filigree.

We hope this new book will give you much pleasure.

The authors

Prepared designs

Paper quilling requires expertise in only a few basic shapes, with the coils being the most important part. Every craft needs practice—so too does paper quilling. This book includes with each design the materials and instructions necessary to assemble them.

The instructions are given in table form (see examples below), with the first column **(C)** listing the types of coils required. The second column **(L)** shows the length of paper strips needed in centimetres. The third column **(Q)** shows the number of each type of coil needed to make the design. The fourth column **(W)** indicates the width of the strips of quilling paper.

The amounts shown have been based on the designs being worked by hand. If you are using a quilling tool or a toothpick, shorten the length of the paper strip by approximately 2 cm (¾″).

The designs are described from top to bottom and from left to right. Symmetrical shapes are described from the centre of the design and all other designs are described in the most workable form.

1a From left to right and from top to bottom of illustration 1:

1				**2**				**3**				**4**				**5**				**6**				**7**			
C	**L**	**Q**	**W**	**C**	**L**	**Q**	**W**	**C**	**L**	**Q**	**W**	**C**	**L**	**Q**	**W**	**C**	**L**	**Q**	**W**	**C**	**L**	**Q**	**W**	**C**	**L**	**Q**	**W**
14	12	1	3	2	48	8	5	14	24	1	7	14	24	7	3	14	24	1	7	14	24	1	3	14	24	1	7
15	24	6	3	14	12	8	5	14	24	4	5	14	6	6	3	14	6	8	5	28	49	6	3	14	24	6	5
				7	6	4	3	14	12	4	5	14	12	6	3	17	12	8	3	14	20	1	3	14	12	12	3
								14	6	12	3					4	12	4	3	28	24	6	3	14	6	18	1½
								14	24	4	1½					3	6	4	3	14	67	7	3				
																14	24	4	5								

Star-shaped frame made with two complete strips

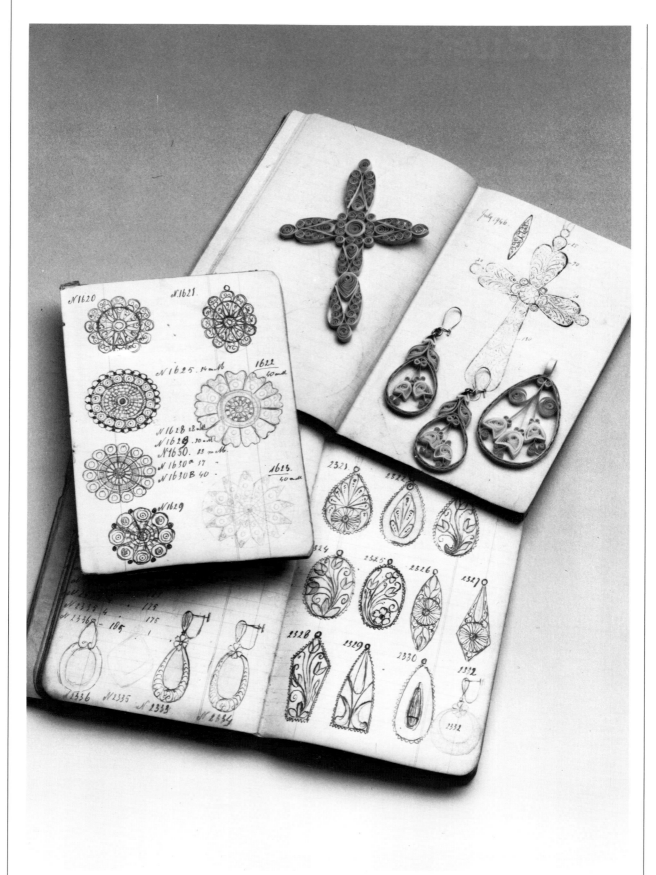

Quilled jewellery made from some traditional silver filigree designs in old silversmith's books

Interview with a silversmith

Researching the art of filigree in the Netherlands brought us to the town of Schoonhoven where we found one of the last silversmiths still practising on a daily basis, Mr Kuyf. He loaned us some old books from which we have reproduced a number of designs (see the illustrations on the opposite page and on page 19). Some of the designs have been reproduced exactly but others gave inspiration to our own compositions. Because paper is not as versatile as silver the designs have to be adapted occasionally, but that does not mean that they are any less beautiful.

How old is the technique of silver filigree and are there any other countries where this art is practised?
We know that Indonesia, Italy, Yugoslavia and even the ancient Egyptians all mastered the art of silver filigree. We are sure that this art has been practised for many centuries.

Decorations of silver filigree have been used in many traditional costumes. Do they also have a symbolic meaning?
The costumes worn by the people of Zeeland [a province of the Netherlands] featured silver filigree on the men's trousers and on the women's dresses. In some areas these decorations were symbolic, but mostly they were used as decoration. Silver filigree was also used to make clasps for bibles, but in the main it was used as a decorative technique.

How many silversmiths used to make silver filigree in days gone by, and how many would still be making it now?
In earlier days when silver filigree was popular, two-thirds of Schoonhoven's silversmiths would have been engaged in making it, but now there are only two or three. This is partly due to a lack of interest and education [on the part of

silversmiths]. There is still occasional talk about silver filigree but there do not seem to be any students of the art. If this continues it will become a dying art.

Is this development due to a lack of interest on the part of the consumer?
Partly, but in Italy where larger quantities are produced there is still a market for silver filigree. Consumer interest is of course very important, as can be seen in the revival in antique brooches. Also the interest in paper quilling is creating renewed interest in silver filigree.

You use silver in these decorations. How pure is it?
In the Netherlands there are two qualities: the first is 925/1000, which is used to make silver filigree; the second is 835/1000, mainly used for parts that receive a lot of wear and tear. The higher the purity, the softer the metal. To harden silver copper is usually added.

Is the silvermark in your decorations your own?
The mark that the silversmith adds is the master mark. Each silversmith gets his own master mark when he graduates. All jewellery made [in the Netherlands] is inspected by a control board. The amount of silver is verified and the item is marked with a quality stamp. In the Netherlands customers can always be assured of the quality of the product.

Is this the same in other countries?
In Germany 800/1000 is used. This will be used in the Netherlands soon to make cutlery. In Germany 930/1000 is also used—this is slightly higher in quality. Imports, especially those from Spain, do not always have the quality that is required here by law. The qualities that [other countries'] factories use don't have to

correspond. The controls used, also those used in other countries, will give the silver quality up to one-thousandth of a measure.

Is it possible to gauge the age of an object from the master mark?
Yes, here in Schoonhoven stamps have been used since 1629. These days stamps are used to mark the control, the year, quality, factory and master mark, making it a relatively simple exercise to accurately date the article and find the creator.

Which method do you use to make filigree decorations?
We use silver wire which we either manufacture ourselves or purchase, depending on what it is to be used for. A wire of 1 mm thickness is unravelled to 0.5 mm thickness. This is then cut to the right size and bent into the desired shape by hand or with a tool. This shape is called a frame. Very fine silver wire (filigree) is worked to fit snugly inside the frame. When the design is completed it is soldered into the frame. This is done by sprinkling very fine solder together with a borax mix across the frame. It is then heated and soldered. Filigree is always soldered flat. If further shaping is required the design can then be bent into shape, making it into a brooch or hanger. There are many ways of using filigree. In Schoonhoven there are actually Jewish steeples decorated with filigree.

You have a button here that is very dull. Does it still need to be finished?
Yes, that is correct. This button has been in the flame and been soldered. You can see a residue on it which was caused by the borax powder, the protectant against oxidisation. Silver that is oxidised can't be soldered. The borax residue is removed with a sulphur mixture. The piece is then put in an oven at a specified temperature to allow the silver to rise to the top. When it has cooled a little it is whitened; this dissolves the copper, leaving the finest silver. Filigree work needs to be as white as possible.

Do you ever take orders or make custom-designed jewellery?

The filigree in costume jewellery is always traditional in design, although there are differences between the Catholic and the Protestant costumes, especially in the pieces used in trousers. The Catholic costume jewellery is a lot more sober than the Protestant. On the question of custom-designed jewellery: being a silversmith you should be able to make anything. Although clock frames are made [commercially] only in England and France they can also be made in Schoonhoven—and Mr Kuyf showed us several very beautiful examples.

Have any drawings of silver filigree been saved from historic times?
In some museums some old drawings can still be found and here in Schoonhoven are some very old work books that we handle very carefully. The oldest book I have goes back to 1880. There are very few books from before that date, probably due to several fires in the town. There is practically nothing to be found about gold filigree; however, any design that can be made in silver filigree can also be made in gold. Working with gold filigree is quite different to working with silver filigree as the gold is much stiffer and more difficult to work with.

How do you see the differences and similarities between silver and paper filigree?
It is very exciting to see people using paper filigree as a hobby. It is an introduction to something very creative. You can do a lot of things with some very simple materials. Silver filigree is simple to do—you just use some pliers and your fingers. Paper filigree just uses fingers and a bit of glue. My wife and daughter too are enjoying working with paper filigree. They recently made a star from paper which I copied and made in silver filigree. The difference between paper and silver filigree lies in the way the materials spring back after bending.

Mr Kuyf's shop is situated at 13 Kazerneplein in Schoonhoven, near the Saint Andrieshuis Clock Museum.

Materials

1 Quilling paper in strips 3 mm (⅛") wide is available from craft shops. You could cut the strips yourself, but they need to be exact in size, as even a millimetre difference in width will cause your design to be uneven. Cutting the strips yourself is a time-consuming exercise, and even one-tenth of a millimetre difference in width when glued to a flat base will give an uneven finish. Nor is it always possible to get the right sort of paper in the necessary colour combinations.

2 A good quality transparent or matt craft glue.

3 Toothpicks or satay sticks for applying glue.

4 Steel ruler.

5 Dressmaker's pins.

6 Quilling tool.

7 A bodkin can be made into a quilling tool by cutting off the eye and pushing a cork or wooden stopper onto the end.

8 Tweezers with sharp points.

9 Small sharp craft knife.

10 Paper scissors.

11 Quilling template with various sized circles.

12 Quilling board with graph paper.

Quilling board

To make the quilling board you will need some strong cardboard, three sheets of graph paper and some clear Contact. From the centre of the graph paper draw concentric circles of varying sizes. With a ruler draw lines through the centres of the

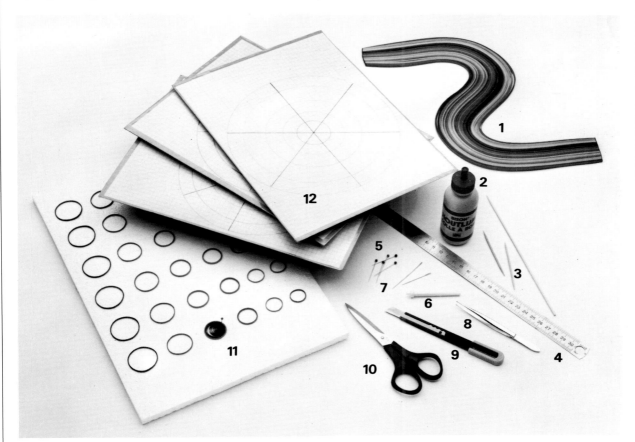

3 Quilling boards, template with circles of varying sizes, scissors and other quilling materials

circles, dividing each circle into five, six or eight equal parts. Place the graph paper on the cardboard and cover in clear Contact. These quilling boards are used to assemble a symmetrical design before it is glued to the backing.

Quilling template

This is a helpful pattern board that can be easily made. Take a piece of polystyrene foam approximately 30 cm (12″) square and at least 1 cm (⅜″) thick. The patterns are made from paper circles, using paper strips cut in half, approximately 1.5 mm (¹⁄₁₆″) wide. Roll the paper strip around a coin or other small circular object and glue the end securely in place. Make 4 to 6 circles of each size and glue them securely to the polystyrene board.

The quilling template can be used to make the spirals with the offset centres. Make a spiral from a strip of paper but do not glue the end. Put this into one of the circles and let it spring back. The spiral will not become larger than the size of the circle will allow. Apply glue to the end of the spiral and press the end against the side of the spiral. Place a pin into the centre of the spiral and pull it gently to the side, towards the point where the spiral is glued. Push the pin into the quilling template and apply glue where the pin meets the side of the spiral. Let the glue dry. Twist the pin around several times before removing to prevent pulling the coil out of shape.

Extra materials

Cardboard, cards, empty cardboard rolls, toilet roll centres, towel rolls, small pebbles, corks, cottonwool balls, styrofoam beads, small boxes, et cetera, will all come in very handy. Beads, sequins, paints and other colourful materials, earring clips, brooch clips, nylon thread and many other materials are available from craft and hobby shops.

Quilling paper

All the designs in this book were made using quilling strips from the Dutch company Comar bv, Waalwyk (illustration 4). Equivalent paper is available from craft shops in other countries.

Quilling strips are available in 1.5 mm, 3 mm, 5 mm and 7 mm widths (¹⁄₁₆″, ⅛″, ³⁄₁₆″, ¼″)

Working with 1.5 mm (¹⁄₁₆″) strips will require some practice. The 5 and 7 mm (³⁄₁₆″, ¼″) strips are very suitable for use by young children.

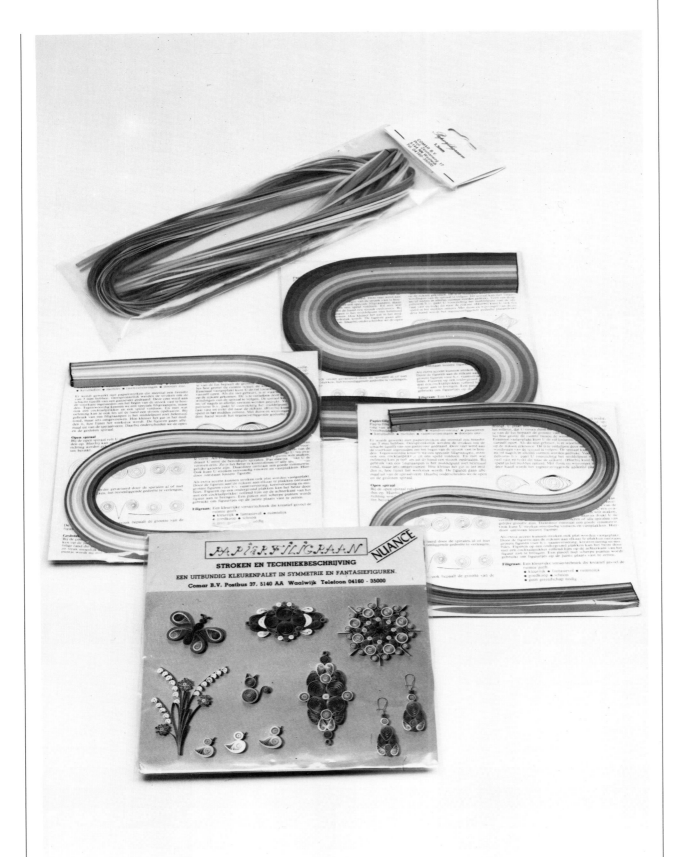

4   A variety of paper quilling strips

Basic shapes

The basic shapes used in quilling are all made up from rolled coils. Coils are classified as either open coils or closed coils.

Open coils (illustration 5)

To make an open coil, the paper strips are rolled either from one end or from both ends. Rolling clockwise or anticlockwise will create different effects. The shapes can then be varied by glueing the coils together and lengthening or folding the strips. The length of the strip of paper will determine the size of the finished coil.

Examples of open coils

1 *Single open coil*
Starting at one end, roll the paper strip into a coil and leave approximately 2 cm (¾″) free at the end.

2 *V shape*
Fold the paper strip in half and curl both ends in opposite directions.

3 *Closed V shape*
Roll the paper strip the same as the V shape and glue the strip together in the centre.

4 *Open heart shape*
Fold the paper strip in half and curl both ends inwards towards each other.

5 *Closed heart shape*
Fold the paper strip in half and curl both ends towards each other; glue the coils together.

6 *Scroll*
Roll the paper strip from both ends towards the middle, leaving the middle piece straight or slightly curved.

5   Basic shapes: open coils

7   *Opposite spiral*
Roll the paper strip from both ends, but in opposite directions.

8   *Double coil*
Fold the strip of paper, leaving one end longer than the other. Roll both ends in the same direction. The folded end can be glued if desired, similar to the V shape coil.

9   *Opposite coil*
Work the same as the double coil, but roll the short end towards the inside.

10   *Double coil with a small diamond, rolled to the inside or outside*
Fold the paper strip in the middle and roll both ends to the outside or the inside, leaving several centimetres (a couple of inches) from the centre unfolded. Apply glue 1 cm (⅜") below the fold and apply pressure to the fold, forming a small diamond shape.

11 *Half a harp*
Fold a paper strip in half and roll both ends together. The inside of the strip will require less paper than the outside, thus causing a loop to form below the fold.

12 *Triple coil*
Fold a paper strip in half and roll each end to the outside or the inside to approximately half way, then roll the double strip back towards the rolled ends.

Closed coils (illustration 10)

The closed coil is made in a slightly different way. The paper strip is torn to the required length by hand, which creates a slightly rough edge which is easier to glue. Roll the strip of paper leaving a small straight piece at the end. At the very end of this piece apply a small amount of glue with a toothpick (illustration 6). Holding the coil between thumb and forefinger attach the end of the strip in a loop (illustration 7). The length of the loop determines the size of the coil. The larger the loop the larger the distance between the rolled strips in the coil.

Once the glue has set lay the coil down and it will spring open (illustration 8). If it fails to open it probably means that a small amount of glue has found its way into the coil. This can be rectified by running a pin through the coil. The coil can then be formed into any shape with the fingers or fingernails (illustration 9).

6   Applying glue

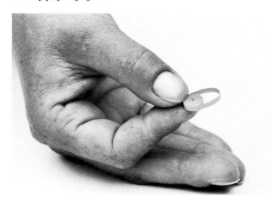

7   The end of the strip is attached in a loop

8   The coil is ready to be formed into shape and glued to the background

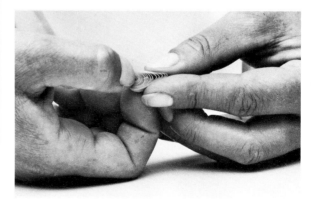

9   Making a teardrop

Colourplate 2: Jewellery copied from old silver filigree designs

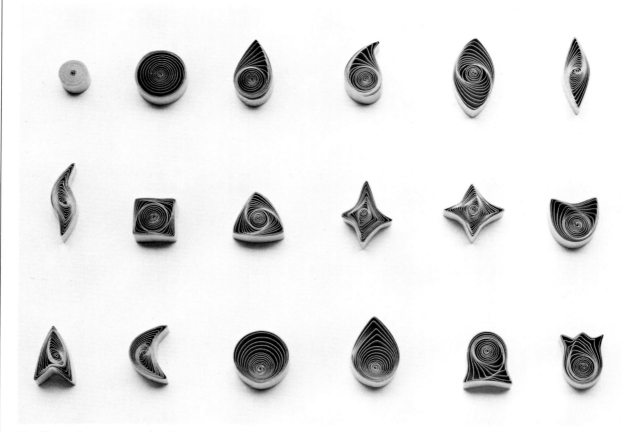

10   Basic shapes: closed coils

Examples of closed coils

13   *Tight coil*
Roll the strip of paper as tightly as possible and glue the end.

14   *Loose coil*
Roll the strip of paper leaving a small straight piece at the end. Apply glue with a toothpick and attach the end to the coil with a loop. The larger the size of the loop the looser the coil.

15   *Teardrop*
Make a loose coil. Hold the centre carefully with one finger or a pin; with the other hand hold the side of the coil. Pull the centre towards the edge and pinch into a point with thumb and first finger.

16   *Flame*
Make a teardrop, pinch the end and bend it in the opposite direction to the circle.

17 *Oval*
Make a loose coil and flatten slightly between thumb and first finger.

18 *Diamond*
Same as the oval but pinch both ends sharply.

19 *Leaf*
Same as for the oval but pinch the ends in opposite directions.

20 *Square*
Make a loose coil and squeeze with thumb and forefinger at both ends, at the same time forming a square.

21 *Triangle*
Make a loose coil, press coil with finger and thumb of one hand and finger of the other hand at the same time, forming it into a triangle.

22 *Holly leaf*
Make a loose coil, press evenly with the nails of both the thumbs and the forefingers. Make sure the coil has been wound very loosely to ensure there is adequate spacing between the layers. This shape does not need to be very even.

23 *Star*
This is made the same as the holly leaf, but make sure the points are even.

24 *Flower petal*
Make a loose coil and press with fingernail to make a rounded indentation at the top of the coil.

25 *Arrow*
Make a flower petal and press to a point on the side opposite to the rounded indentation.

26 *Half moon*
Make a loose coil. Press the coil flat and pull both points to one side.

27 *Loose coil with offset centre*
Make a loose coil and pull the centre to one side. Apply a small amount of glue to the back. Let the glue dry before continuing work.

28 *Leaf shape with offset centre*
Make a loose coil, but when glue has dried pinch top into leaf shape.

These last two shapes are easier to make using the quilling template (page 12).

29 *Bell*
Make a flower petal, pinching the ends and twisting them to the outside.

30 *Tulip*
Make a bell; while pinching the ends press towards the centre to create an extra point.

Extending basic shapes

1 *Open loose coil with offset centre*
Using a quilling template make a loose coil with an offset centre. When the glue is dry, remove the pin by turning it in a circular motion. Lift the coil out of the template. With pointed scissors cut the outside layer or layers of paper. The part of the coil that remains uncut is framed within a fan shape.

2 *Open leaf shape with offset centre*
As for the previous shape, make a loose coil in the quilling template and shape it into a leaf (number 28). With scissors cut one or more layers of paper at the fold.

11 From left to right and from top to bottom of colourplate 3:

1			
C	**L**	**Q**	**W**
14	15	1	3
14	24	4	3
17	24	4	3
5	24	4	3
5	12	4	3

2			
C	**L**	**Q**	**W**
14	15	1	3
17	8	22	3
17	12	8	3
—	—	—	—

Two frames made with milled strips

3			
C	**L**	**Q**	**W**
14	24	1	3
14	6	6	3
27	49	6	3
3	24	6	3
14	12	6	3

4			
C	**L**	**Q**	**W**
14	8	1	3
14	6	3	3
19	12	2	3
19	8	2	3
24	12	5	3

An oval frame

5			
C			

Frame made with milled strips. Fill the centre with open loose coils made from paper strips 4 cm long and 3 mm wide (1½″ × ⅛″).

6			
C	**L**	**Q**	**W**
14	15	1	3
14	8	4	3
2	24	4	3
17	12	4	3
17	8	4	3

Colourplate 3: Quilled designs with and without frames

3 *Loose coil with offset centre and two loops*

This is a difficult shape to give a name to, but it is made as follows: Using the quilling template make a coil with an offset centre. With a second pin press several of the paper strips together, directly opposite the first pin. This creates a figure-eight shape. Apply glue to the second pin and spread the glue around approximately 2 mm. When the glue has dried remove the pins and lift the coil out of the template. Cut the glued strips so that the glue holds the tips of the loops together.

4 *Centre-cut strip*

To give an extra dimension to your work, cut a strip of paper lengthwise down the middle. Both sides can be rolled into loose coils. Glue one coil to the background and leave the other coil free.

5 *Fish*

From one strip of paper make a closed coil. Pull the centre completely to one side. With the thumb and forefinger of the other hand form the opposite end into the shape of a tail. Holding the tail end apply glue to the side of the coil, directly in front of the bulge. Let the glue dry while holding the shape. When the glue has dried the tail can be pushed into shape.

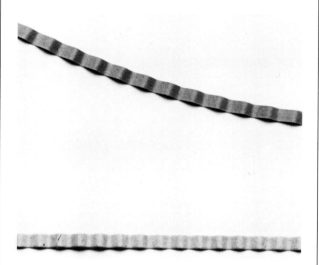

12   Straight and semi-round milled strips

6 *Milled strips* (illustration 12)

Several of the designs in this book have been made using milled strips. They are generally used to strengthen and to add volume to a frame (see page 38 and the lower illustration on page 35).

To make milled strips you need a device with two cogs that are neither too deep nor too sharp. The cogs on a Lego Technics system are very suitable.

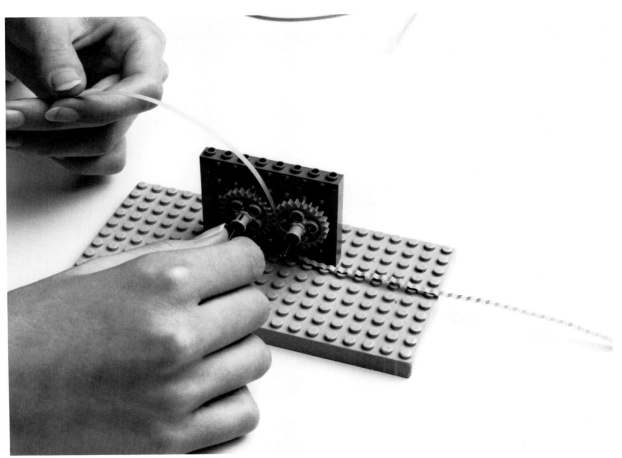

13 Making milled strips with a Lego Technics system

Pass the strip of paper between the two cogs making sure you do not pull the strip or you will lose the milled effect (illustration 13).

Glue the milled strip to a plain strip of paper by applying glue only to the bumps, then gently pressing the milled strip to the flat strip. Cut the plain strip of paper to size. Do not glue one milled strip to another milled strip—always glue a flat strip between the milled strips.

Two or three layers of milled and flat strips will make a sturdy frame.

The cogs of the Lego Technics system give a straight finish to the milled strips. If you wanted a different effect you could use another cog system such as a hand drill (illustration 14). The milled strips would not be suitable for making frames, but could be used on a flat background to make rounded or curved lines.

14 Making milled strips with a hand drill

Colourplate 4: A beautiful example of a traditional quilling design

Colourplate 5: Some modern quilling designs

Freeform shapes (illustration 15)

Strips of paper can simply be folded or bent to any shape desired and then glued to the background. Freeform strips are beautifully suited to making leaves, grass and birds. You can make a frame for your design by glueing strips of paper to the background.

1 *Extended leaf*
Two strips of paper of uneven length glued together at the ends will make an extended leaf.

15   Freeform shapes

2 *Grass*

By folding a strip of paper in small sections it is possible to create the illusion of grass. Glue these to a flat strip of paper and they will stand up.

3 *Birds*

Take small strips of paper, fold in the centre and slightly bend the sides.

4 *Spirals*

Wind strips of paper diagonally around a toothpick or a satay stick.

Colourplate 6: Wall decoration of half harps made with multiple strips (page 32)

Quilling techniques

Quilling is based on the technique of rolling narrow strips of paper into coils. This can be done by hand or with the help of a quilling tool. For beginners a quilling tool can make life a lot easier.

Making a coil using a tool

You can wind the strips of paper using a quilling tool, a toothpick, a satay stick or an embroidery needle.

A quilling tool is shaped like a pen with a slit in the end. Slide the paper into the slit of the quilling tool and roll it around to form a coil (illustration 17).

Using a toothpick or other implement will require a slightly different approach as the strip of paper cannot be fastened into a slit as in the quilling tool.

Hold the strip of paper on the top of the index finger and press the toothpick into the end of the strip (illustration 18). Pressing the toothpick into the paper will raise the end of the paper strip slightly; it can then be twisted around the toothpick with the thumb and rolled into a coil. The end of the rolled coil is then glued as described on page 16.
The disadvantage of using a quilling tool is that it always leaves a small hole in the centre of the coil.

17　Winding a coil with a quilling tool

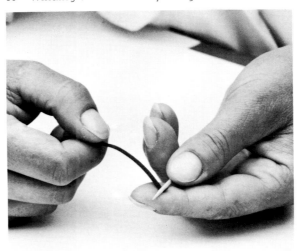

16　To prevent the toothpick sticking to the background and the glue drying out it is a good idea to rest the tooth pick in the glue container

18　Starting a coil with a toothpick

Coils made with a quilling tool are easily recognised because the centre of the coil is not circular but folded.

Making a coil without a tool

Take a strip of paper in one hand and softly round the end with your fingernail or the end of your scissors. Press the end of the paper strip with the nail of your index finger and make a small fold, no larger than 0.5 mm. Repeat this, making a second fold behind the first one. Now start rolling the paper between your thumb and index finger (illustration 19).

At this stage you can move the coil to the other hand without it springing apart. Continue rolling, using the other thumb and index finger as a guide.

Making a coil in this way requires a certain amount of practice, but using this method you can make very small coils successfully (illustration 20).

Once the coil is finished, whether you glue it or not, it can be put down on a flat surface, where it will spread out. You may notice that some of the outside windings are close together. This can give quite a good effect, but if you prefer you can even the circles by turning the centre slightly.

This spreading out of the coil is called expansion. Ideally the coil will expand with a flat surface, but because the pressure exerted by the fingers is not always even, a coil can sometimes expand telescopically. That is, when you place the coil on a flat surface the centre or the sides will rise. To prevent this happening you may need to apply a small amount of glue to the centre of the coil before placing it in position.

19 Making a coil with a tool will ensure a finer structure

20 A coil made without a tool

Using quilling strips in different widths

Most quilling is done using paper strips 3 mm (⅛″) wide. It can be very challenging to use paper strips in different widths. The variation of widths in a design can be very interesting and can give a greater depth to the subject. Do remember that it may take a little extra care to achieve an interesting effect.

Using strips of paper wider or thinner than the standard 3 mm (⅛″) size will not change the size of the design. A wider strip of paper will give the design greater depth, but it will not be larger. It is the length of the strip of paper and the size of the loop that determines the size of the coil.

You may find that using thinner strips of paper will lead to smaller and finer designs than when you are using wider strips. This may be because a strip 1.5 mm (¹⁄₁₆″) wide will be much harder to roll into a coil than the standard size strip of paper. Strips of 1.5 mm (¹⁄₁₆″) paper are very suitable for making greeting cards, as they will not flatten out so much when they are sent through the mail.

21 Three-dimensional quilled designs

Half harps made with multiple strips

Quilling is usually very fine work because the basic shapes are small. If you wish to cover a larger area you will need many more or much larger basic shapes.

It is possible to make larger shapes by using several paper strips at the same time. These paper strips can be cut straight from the packet leaving the glued ends together (illustration 22). You can gather a number of strips and glue them together at the ends yourself. You can also glue the paper strips at one end and leave some or all of the strips loose at the other end (illustration 23/2). When the paper strips remain glued at both ends, twisting them creates the effect of a variation of the half harp (illustration 23/1).

22 Cutting a bunch of strips from the packet

23 Several variations of the half harp

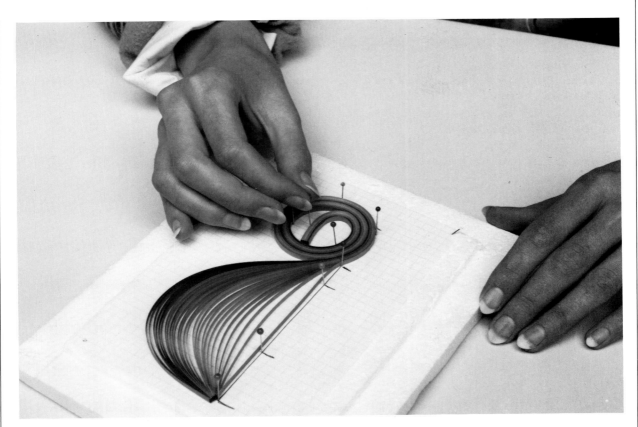

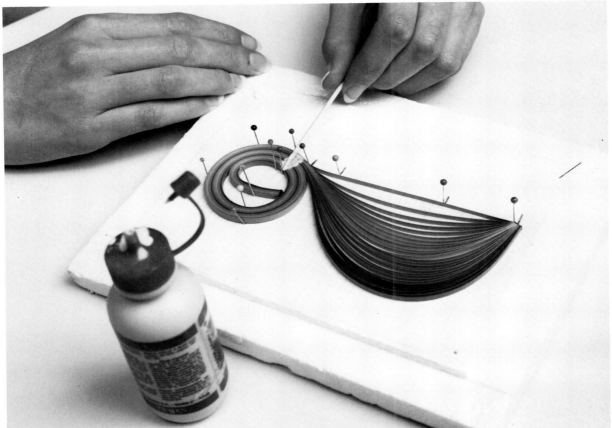

24 Attaching and glueing a half harp

A coil made from several strips of paper cannot be folded and will spring back when released. To hold it in place you will have to apply glue evenly to the side of the strips. To roll the coil you will find that a round aid is very helpful. The greater the number of strips the larger the circumference of the aid will need to be.

To glue the side it would be simpler to pin the coil to a piece of polystyrene. A small piece of graph paper attached to the polystyrene would be helpful in determining the size and make it easier to make all the coils the same size (illustration 24).

If the inside turn of the coil is not glued it is possible to twist the beginning of the coil with a pair of tweezers in the opposite direction. This createst an effect inside the coil similar to the fan effect of the loose ends (illustration 23/4).

This basic shape made up of several strips used together can give rise to a myriad variations (illustration 23).

If the strips are glued at the beginning of the coil the ends of each separate strip can be left to fan out separately. These ends can then be rolled individually into different sized coils (illustration 25).

Using a few of these basic shapes in combination with flat glued strips can create some very exciting designs (pages 25 and 28).

Tying a knot in a bunch of paper strips can make a fascinating variation to a design (page 25).

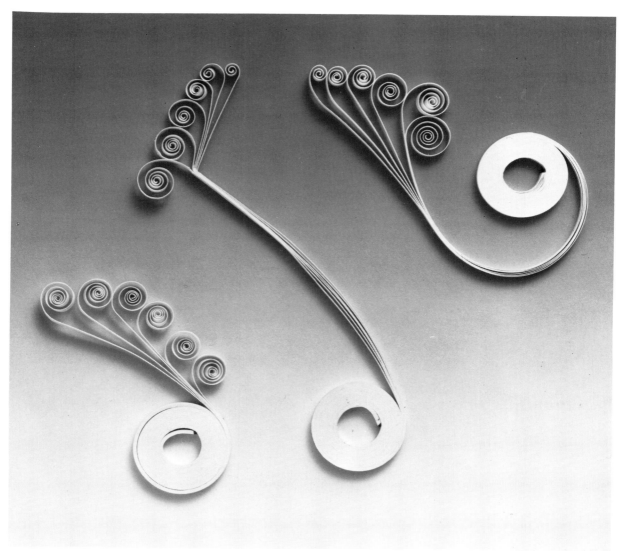

25   Some more variations to half harps

25a Two quilled pieces made with frames

Filling in outlines

On pages 28 and 37 you will find examples of filling in outlines with paper quilling. One piece is made using several basic shapes in a composition of lines and forms. The other shows two ladies dressed in the fashion of the nineteenth century. This wall hanging was made by Mr and Mrs De Vries from Ochten. With much patience and also a lot of pleasure it took them three and a half months to make this.

Choosing basic shapes to fit into the lines of the pattern has accentuated the beauty of the subject. The absolute precision used throughout the making has made this into a true masterpiece of quilling.

26 Fashionable ladies from the late nineteenth century in paper filigree

Colourplate 7: This lovely example shows clearly how extensive are the possibilities of quilling

Frames

Frames are often used to increase the strength of the quilled piece and quite often to hold the work together.

Paper quilling uses frames (illustration 30) not necessarily for greater strength but also to enhance the subject or accentuate details or different sections.

There are several methods of making frames.

Circular, square, oblong or triangular shapes are easily made using everyday objects as templates for particular shapes. You could use lids from cosmetic bottles, cigarette lighters, sticks, children's blocks, et cetera, providing they are smooth and have no protruding edges. The frame must be able to slide off easily. Wrap the paper strip around the object several times, applying a small amount of glue to each twist (illustrations 28 and 29). Glue the end of the strip and slide the paper frame off the object. This method is particularly useful for small frames that are even in shape.

27   Example of a decorated frame

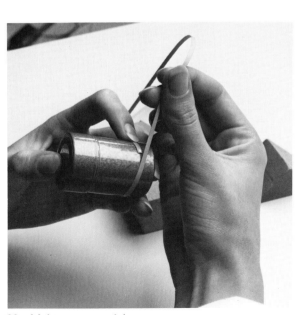

28   Making a round frame

29   Making a square frame

30 A variety of frames

Colour plate 8: Ikebana shapes and decorated buttons (see page 46)

Making larger and irregular shaped frames requires a different method. Start by drawing an outline of the required shape. Graph paper or measuring paper are very suitable for this. Attach the paper to a sheet of polystyrene with pins at the corners.

The easiest shapes to start with are angled or rounded shapes that point to the outside of the paper. Press a pin into each corner. On curves insert pins at regular intervals (illustration 31). The more pins you use the more easily the paper strip will follow the curves.

A frame is built up of several layers of paper, usually four. Determine the area of the shape first. Next, glue the required length of paper strips together, making sure the strip will be long enough to wrap around the shape four times.

Half a centimetre (⅜″) from the beginning fold the paper strip and wrap it around a pin on a corner. Using another pin fix the end of the strip. Now wrap the rest of the strip around the other pins, making a fold in the strip at each pin. This is done to prevent the paper strips from sagging. When you reach the first pin again, attach the strip with glue. The folded piece at the beginning of the strip can now be glued down also. Continue winding the paper strip and glueing it to the previous strip at each corner, taking care not to spill glue on the drawing.

31 Attaching a flat strip of paper to a milled strip

When you have wound the strip around a sufficient number of times tear the end and glue it.

The method used for shapes that point or curve to the inside is similar to the previous method. At the second and

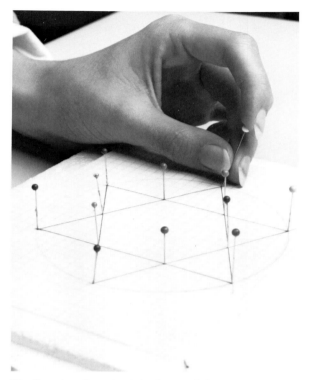

following turns the paper strip between the previous strip and the pin will tend to bend to the inside (illustrations 32 and 33). Take the pin out of the polystyrene for a second, adjust the strip and press the pin back in the same place again.

So far we have concentrated on a frame that has been made with the layers close together, giving the frame a rather solid look. A very attractive and definitely more sturdy alternative is to add some ribbed strips or some extra basic shapes to the frame (illustration 30). Around this, thicker than the first frame, another frame of straight strips could be added.

The inside of the frame must then be filled in. Leave the pins in place to hold the shape. The frame will need to contain enough basic shapes connected to each other that when the pins are removed the frame will retain its shape (see the star on page 6).

When the frame is finished remove the pins, twisting them carefully to avoid disturbing the design, in case some glue has stuck to the pins.

32 Pressing the pins into the worksheet

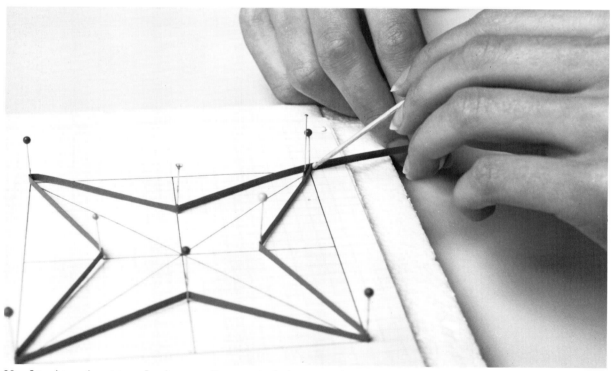

33 Attaching the strips. Apply a small amount of glue at each corner

Protecting quilled designs

Objects made from metals such as silver and gold need very little protection to prevent discolouration. Paper quilling, however, can quite easily be damaged or discoloured by light, moisture and other natural elements. If the fragile designs are handled a lot the paper quilling can lose its shape and therefore its attractiveness. When you have spent a lot of time creating a quilled design you may want to protect it against these influences.

Paper quilling can be protected in several ways. You will have to choose whether you want to protect the paper strips before using them or after the article has been quilled. Each method has its advantages. Coating the paper strips prior to using them has the disadvantage of the amount of time required for them to dry, but you could organise this before you plan to work and keep a store of coated paper strips.

Different methods of protecting paper strips before use

1 *Spraying with a sealant*
Pin the required number of paper strips to a sheet of polystyrene and spray one side with a fixative or non-yellowing clear varnish. When the strips are dry, turn them over and repeat the process on the other side. Make sure the strips are thoroughly dry before use.

2 *Dipping in a liquid flexible acrylic finish* (illustration 34)
Use a container long enough to hold the

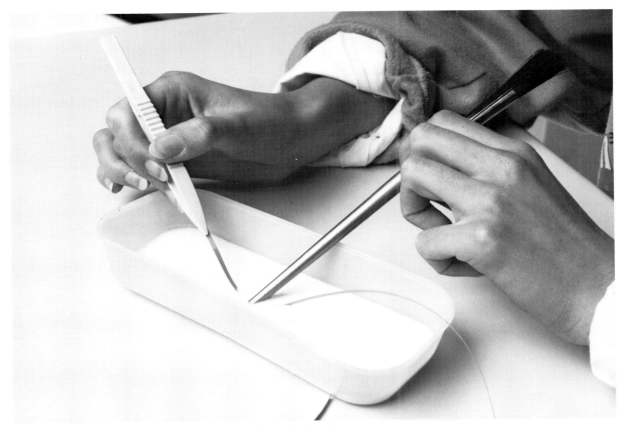

34 Dipping a paper strip into a container of acrylic finish

paper strips. Pour in an amount of finish and add a small amount of water (water is added to diminish the gloss of the sealer). Use 1 part of water to 10 parts of finish. Using tweezers pick up a strip of paper and pull its complete length through the finish. You may need to use a fork to hold it down. Take the end of the strip and wrap it around a coathanger (illustration 35). Make sure the strips are far enough apart that they do not stick to each other. Leave the paper strips to dry for at least 24 hours, making sure they don't feel sticky. The layer of finish may mean that it takes a little longer for the glue to dry and stick properly when working with the treated strips.

The advantage of both these methods is that the whole paper strip is covered in finish.

Protecting the design after it is made

Clear nail polish, varnish or spray enamel can be used to protect a design after it is made (illustration 36). The design will dictate the protection necessary.

For designs that are glued to a base, such as boxes and wallhangings, it would be better to use a spray can so that the base is sprayed with the finish at the same time. Window ornaments, jewellery, Christmas decorations and other forms of quilling without a base are probably best painted with nail enamel or other enamel finishes applied to the quilled design with a brush. To prevent the design sticking to the work surface a small piece of chicken wire makes a fine base (illustration 36).

Use a fine paintbrush with long bristles. Hold the design with a pair of tweezers

35 Drying the prepared paper strips

36 Protecting a design with clear nail polish

while painting it. Make sure to clean the brush thoroughly after use with methylated spirits, acetone or mineral turpentine. When brushing on a finish use it sparingly to prevent it sticking between the windings of the coil and closing up the design. The design must be turned regularly to ensure even distribution of the finish and to prevent it sticking to the background. Most finishes will slightly alter the colour of the paper or add a slight sheen.

Ikebana shapes

Once you start quilling you will look at your surroundings in a different way, continually searching for designs and ideas that can be used for flat as well as three-dimensional paper quilling. Because flower designs are very well suited to paper quilling, floral decoration can be a source of inspiration.

Ikebana is a very special form of floral art. This Japanese art of flower decoration, which uses a stunningly effective simple combination of lines, colours and shapes, was a fount of inspiration for the simple three-dimensional designs on page 40. The flower compositions are all made on a base which forms the foundation but also becomes part of the whole design.

The base is very simple to make. Glue a number of paper strips together lengthwise, usually three or four strips. The strips should be a background colour, not too bright, or they will overshadow the total design.

Make a closed coil, tightly wound, and push the outside windings slightly up. This will form a dish shape.

You could also fold the end of the paper strip and wind the rest of the strip around that. This will form an oval shape. The longer the length of the first fold the longer the shape of the oval. The design will sit on top of or inside this base. The size of the base is very important in relation to the size of the design.

These Ikebana-like designs require just a few of the basic shapes to catch the attention.

It goes without saying that the precision with which the bases are made requires the utmost concentration. The windings of the paper strips need to be totally even for the effect to be shown to its best advantage.

Line motifs

One of the reasons paper quilling appeals to people is the artistry of the lines. In particular the way the distances between the lines can vary is appealing. Just look at the basic shapes of the closed coils (page 17).

Paper strips are also very useful for creating line motifs in a flat base. This also requires evenly worked distances between the lines and neat work is essential for a beautiful result.

As well as the even lines it is also possible to work in angles.

The angles must fit beside each other and be made very evenly.

The paper strips do not necessarily have to be 3 mm (⅛") wide. A combination of different widths in a design can create an interesting effect.

If the paper strips are moistened it is even possible to make wavy lines. This can only be done with paper strips 1 mm (¹⁄₂₄") and 3 mm (⅛") wide. Do not make the waves too wide, as the paper may bubble or tear.

When you cut a bunch of paper strips from a packet it can be used to make line motifs. Usually the packets of paper strips are produced so that a large number of colour combinations can be cut at the same time. It is your choice as to what colour combinations will have the best effect.

One of the most effective uses of line motifs is as wall decorations. The method is simple: cut a bunch of paper strips (approximately 12 to 20) from a packet. Hold this bunch between the thumb and forefinger of the left hand approximately 10 cm (4") from the glued end. With the right hand bend the strips down and pinch the bent strips between the thumb and forefinger of the right hand. Release the left hand and bend the strips to the right. Pinch the strips with the left hand and bend them down. Repeat this several times.

This creates an S shape. The distance between the strips stays even because the top strips are bent in a larger curve than the lower strips.

To fix the strips, or if required to repeat the action, apply some glue to the side of the strips.

It is handy to attach this to a piece of polystyrene, as for the half harp with several strips. The points that are glued must be attached securely and pressed tightly together. Use at least two pins at both sides of the strips.

When the points to be glued are identified (you will need to apply a minimum of 5 mm (³⁄₁₆") of glue) scratch a sharp hobby knife across the spots where the glue is to be applied. Then apply the glue to the full width of the bunch of paper strips. When the glue has dried remove the pins.

Use your imagination to create your own attractive designs using a bunch of paper strips glued to a base (page 2). Remember that this bunch of paper strips does have a clearly visible top and bottom. Take care that the side with the glue is not visible.